BATTLE FOR SAIPAN

1944 PACIFIC D-DAY IN THE MARIANA ISLANDS

DANIEL WRINN

D1521860

CONTENTS

GET YOUR FREE COPY OF WW2: SPIES, SNIPERS AND THE WORLD AT WAR

Never miss a new release by signing up for my free readers group. Learn of special offers and interesting details I find in my research. You'll also get WW2: Spies, Snipers and Tales of the World at War delivered to your inbox. (You can unsubscribe at any time.) Go to danielwrinn.com to sign up.

BREACHING THE MARIANAS

Dawn on June 15, 1944 would be a brutal day. Navy fire support ships off Saipan Island increased the previous day's firing. At 0542, Admiral Richmond Kelly Turner ordered, "Land the landing force." At 0700, the LSTs (Landing Ship, Tank) moved to a thousand yards behind the line of departure.

Troops waiting in the LSTs debarked into LVTs (Landing Vehicle, Tracked). Navy and Marine personnel took their positions with radio gear. They displayed flags to indicate which beach approaches they controlled.

Admiral Turner delayed H-hour for 10 minutes until 0840 to give the boat waves extra time to get into position. After the first wave headed full speed at the beaches, the Japanese were ready. They waited, poised to make the Marine assault units pay a heavy price in blood.

The first assault wave contained LVT [A]s (armored amphibian tractors) with their swiftly firing 75mm guns. Escorted by light gunboats firing 4.5-inch rockets and 40mm guns. The LVTs could negotiate their way through the reef.

But the gunboats could not and had to turn around until they could uncover a passage through the reef.

Farther north at 0600, a diversionary landing was organized off Tanapag harbor by the 2nd, 24th, and 29th Marines. The Japanese were not deceived and didn't rush any reinforcements to the area. But the ruse tied up one complete enemy regiment.

When the LVTs reached the reef, the battle exploded. Water fountained from mortar and artillery shells exploding in every direction. Rifles, machine guns, and small arms fire joined the crescendo as the LVTs ground ashore.

Mayhem spread through the beaches, mainly in the 2nd Marine Division area. A northern current caused the 6th and 8th Marine assault battalions to land five hundred yards too far north. This created a gap between the 2nd and 4th Marine Divisions. Colonel Hogaboom, operations officer of the Expeditionary Troops wrote: "The opposition consisted primarily of artillery and mortar fire from weapons placed in well-deployed positions. Previously registered to cover the beach areas, and fire from small arms, automatic weapons, and anti-boat guns sited to cover the approaches for the nearest landing beaches."

The result was five of the 2nd Marine Division assault unit commanders wounded. Afetan Point, in the middle, was raked by deadly enfilade fire to the left and right. This allowed two battalions of the 23rd and 25th Marines to cross the gap. The original plan was for the assault troops to ride their LVTs to the first objective, the O-1 line. But the surge of enemy fire and natural obstacles prevented this.

A few units in the center of the 4th Division made it through, but fierce enemy resistance pinned them down on the left and right flanks. This prevented the two divisions from making direct contact.

In the 3rd Battalion, 24th Marine Regiment, a young lieutenant recalled his extraordinary experience on the beach when he came ashore: "All around us was chaos and bitter combat. Marine and Jap bodies laid in mangled and grotesque positions. Blasted and burnt-out pillboxes. Burning wrecks of LVTs knocked out by high-velocity Jap fire. The acrid smell of high explosives. Shattered trees. And the churned-up sand littered with discarded equipment."

After his company moved inland a short distance, he experienced the terrifying pre-registered Japanese artillery fire: "Wham! A shell landed right on top of us. I was too surprised to think, but instinctively, we all hit the deck and spread out. Then shells poured down on us: behind, ahead, on both sides, and right in our midst. They rocketed down like a freight train, thundering, and exploding into a deafening roar.

"I realized the first shell bursts we heard were ranging shots. Now the Japs had zeroed in on us, and we were pinned down in a full-fledged barrage. Their fire hit us with pinpoint accuracy, and it wasn't hard to see why: Fifteen hundred feet above us were Jap observation posts honeycombing the crest of Mt. Tapotchau."

That night the lieutenant and his runner shared a foxhole and split watches. Death came close again: "The hours of my watch passed slowly. I leaned over to shake my runner awake. 'It's time for your watch,' I whispered. 'Watch out for that place over there, might be Japs in it. Stay awake.' After that, I rolled over and was asleep in an instant.

"As if it was right away, someone shook me and insisted I wake up. I jerked and bolted upright—your reflexes act faster in combat, and you never entirely go to sleep. I glanced at my watch, and it was almost dawn. I turned to my runner, lying against me asleep. 'Let's go,' I said. 'Pass the word to squad leaders to get set.' But he didn't move. I shook him. Again, he didn't move. He was dead. With all the barbarity that war demands, I rolled him over, took his canteen, and poured the precious water into my own. Then I left him lying there. Dead."

The assault regiments took casualties from constant shelling zeroed in by spotters on high ground. Reinforcing and supply units piled up from the confusion on the landing beaches. Snipers lurked everywhere. The support waves experienced the same deadly enemy fire on their way to the beach. Many LVTs took direct hits, others were flipped over on their sides by waves or enemy fire—spilling equipment and personnel onto the reef. Casualties in both divisions mounted. Evacuating them to the ships was dangerous and difficult. The medical aid station set up ashore was also under enemy fire.

Marine artillery landed in the late afternoon on D-Day to support the infantry. They received deadly-accurate counterbattery fire from the Japanese. General Harry Schmidt, in command of the 4th Division, came ashore at 1930 and later wrote, "The command post during that time did not function very well. It was the hottest spot I was in during the war."

Major James (Jim) Donovan, executive officer of the 1/6 Marines, survived a mortar bombardment with uncanny timing and precision: "We entered a little village called Charan-Kanoa. We had stopped to get some water and were washing up and resting when mortar shells fell on us. We saw a tall smokestack hiding a Japanese forward observer. He was directing fire and looking right down on us. It didn't occur to anyone that someone could be up in that smokestack after all that naval gunfire and everything else fired into the area. But he was sure up there all right. He killed a lot of Marines from G Company that day.

"He caught us without foxholes. We had a false sense of security. We thought we could relax. Wrong. We had to dig holes in a hurry. It's hard to dig a hole when you're lying on your stomach digging with your chin, knees, toes, and elbows. While it's possible to dig a hole that way, we lost more Marines than we should have before someone located that Jap observer. I don't know how tall that smokestack was, but at least two or three stories high. From up there, he saw the entire picture, and he really gave it to us."

At night on D-Day, the Japanese continued to probe Marine positions. Fire from bypassed enemy soldiers and enemy attacks screened by a curtain of civilians. The 6th Marines dealt with the main counterattack on the far-left flank. Over two-thousand Japanese moved south from Gara-pan. And by 2200, they attacked. Led by tanks, they charged, but were met by a wall of fire from 37mm antitank guns, .30-caliber machine guns, and M-1 rifles. It was too much, and they pulled back.

The Japanese retreated, leaving seven hundred men dead and an abandoned tank. The body of the bugler who blew the charge slumped over the open hatch. A bullet had gone straight up his bugle and blew his brains out.

Illumination shells, fired from Navy ships, were vital for the Marine defense that night and on many other nights. Japanese records revealed, "as soon as the night attack units go forward, the enemy points out targets by using large star shells which turned night into day. Thus making the maneuvering of units extremely difficult."

Weary Marines tried to get some sleep along the irregular line of foxholes. Two things were clear: they had forced themselves onto a perilous beachhead through the teeth of fierce enemy fire, and a ferocious battle lay ahead.

While the Marines focused on survival and the immediate ground in front of them, Senior Command regarded the landing's initial success as a culmination of months of planning, organization, and training for a strategic strike on the crucial Japanese stronghold. The opportunity for this sprang from earlier victories in the Central Pacific. The Marine conquest of Tarawa in November 1943, followed by the joint Marine-Army capture of Eniwetok and Kwajalein in the Marshall Islands in February 1944, had broken the ring of Japanese defenses, and set the stage for future operations.

These earlier victories allowed the American operational timetable for the Central Pacific to move up by three months. After discussions on various alternatives (an attack on the Japanese base at Truk). The Joint Chiefs decided on their next objective: the Mariana Islands. There were three principal targets: Saipan, Tinian, and Guam. A bold decision because Saipan was over 1,300 miles from the Marshall Islands and 3,200 miles from Hawaii, but only 1,250 miles from Japan. These islands were linchpins in the defensive line, which the Japanese felt they had to hold after the previous losses in the Southwest and Central Pacific.

Saipan also represented a whole new kind of problem for an American assault. Instead of a small flat coral inlay on an atoll, it was a large island target of seventy-two miles. The terrain varied from swamps to flat cane fields to steep cliffs. The Japanese considered it *their* territory, although it was legally only a mandate provided by the Versailles Treaty's terms after World War I. The Japanese removed all outsiders and started military construction in 1934.

Attacking a formidable objective like Saipan demanded complex planning and a much greater force than previously needed in the Central Pacific. Admiral Raymond A. Spruance was in overall command of the force ordered to invade the Marianas. Admiral Turner was in command of the Amphibious Task Force. Corps Commander, General Holland Smith was tasked with directing the landing forces on Saipan and then on to the neighboring island of Tinian.

The operational plan for the invasion of Saipan was code-named, Forager. It called for an assault on the western side of the island, with the 2nd Marine Division on the left and the 4th Marine Division on the right. The Army's 27th Infantry Division, led by Major General Ralph C. Smith, was held in reserve, ready to be fed into the battle if needed. While both Marine divisions had previously fought as a complete unit, the 27th had experienced only two minor landings (on Makin and Eniwetok islets).

These three divisions trained intensively in Hawaii. General Schmidt's 4th Marine Division trained on Maui. General Watson's 2nd Marine Division on Hawaii Island (Big Island). And Army General Ralph Smith's 27th Infantry Division on Oahu.

These were busy and hard-working months. Replacements arrived to fill gaps left by the recent battle casualties. These men needed to be well-versed in all the complexities of field-work. Most of the replacements were boys fresh from boot camp, ignorant of everything except for the barest essentials. Their weeks consisted of long marches, live fire, field combat problems, obstacle courses, judo, street-fighting, calisthenics, and several lectures on errors made during the recent Namur battle. An added emphasis was placed on how to attack forti-fied positions. They worked with demolition charges of TNT, dynamite, and plastic explosive. They learned to use flamethrowers until they could operate them forward and backward.

In May 1944, the final maneuvers for the practice landings were ready for all three divisions. The operational plan looked efficiently organized on paper. According to a young lieutenant on Maui it looked different: "To us, it was the same old stuff we'd been doing for a year. Filing up from compartments below decks to your assigned boat station. Going over the side. Hurrying down the net to beat the stopwatch and into the heaving LVCP (Landing Craft Vehicle Personnel). Endless hours of circling—wet, hungry, and bored. The K rations tasted like sawdust. The weather only got rougher, and some of the men got so seasick. All of us were soaking wet and so cold.

"When we finally headed back toward the transport and scrambled up over the cargo net, there was a sigh of relief. The next day was the same thing all over again. Only this time, we went ashore. Getting your only pair of socks and shoes wet, wading through the surf, and rushing onto the beach before all the sand mingled inside your shoes. Confusing and conflicting orders flowed down through the chain of command: move on, halt, go here, go there."

The attack force gathered at Pearl Harbor. Over eight hundred ships set out in the armada. Some for direct troop fire support, some for transport, and some (Fast Carrier Task Force) made advance airstrikes and then were tasked with dealing with any attacks the landing would provoke from the Japanese Navy.

General Holland Smith's V Amphibious Corps totaled over 71,000 Marines and Army troops. They sailed on May 25, headed for Saipan. The troops got their final briefings at sea. Maps of the island, based on recent aerial and submarine photographs, estimated 15,000 enemy troops (turned out to be over 30,000) along with their detailed attack plans for two Marine divisions.

Planes launched from American fast carriers on June 11. They softened up enemy targets and attacked Japanese land-based air. Two days later, the main enemy fleet headed to the Marianas for a decisive battle. Then on June 14, the old battle-ships of the US Navy, ready to dish up some payback from the Pearl Harbor disaster, moved in close to Saipan and hammered Japanese defenders with their heavy guns. UDTs (Underwater Demolition Teams) made treacherous swims close to the assault beaches. They checked channels, reefs, and reconnoitered beach defenses. Everything was ready for the landings.

The bloody business of D-Day was only the beginning—a long grueling fight had yet to come.

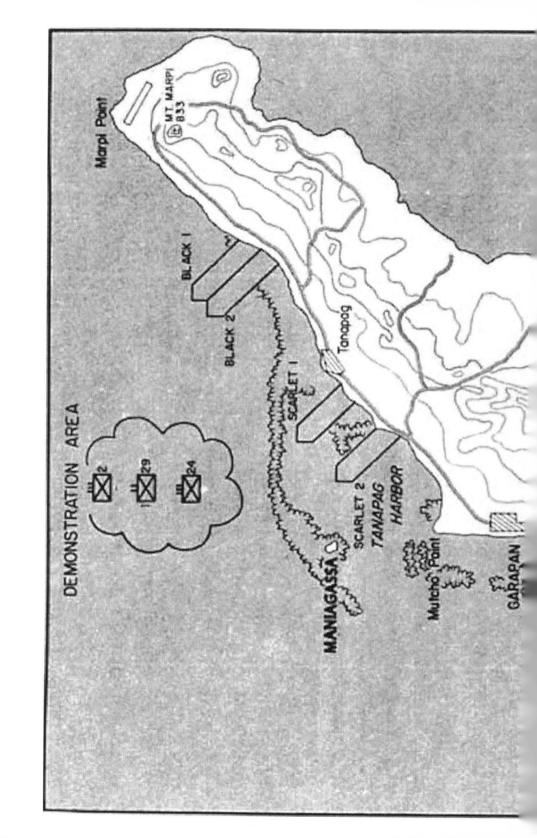

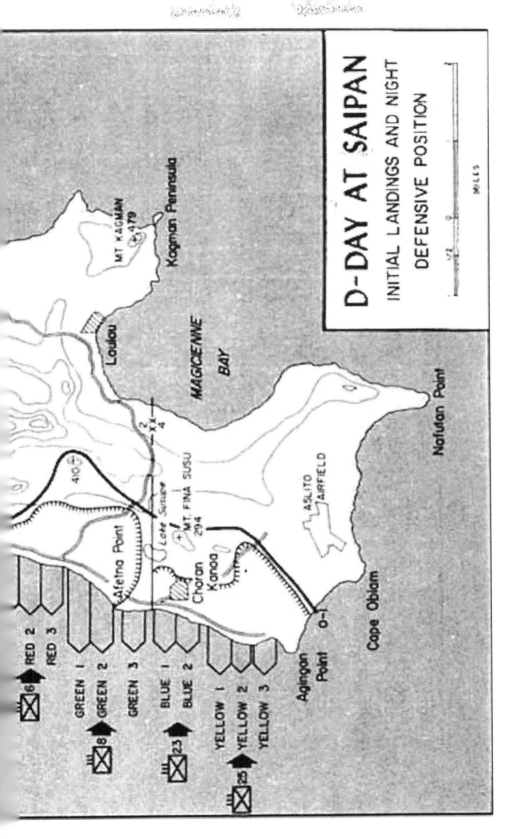

D-DAY AT SAIPAN

INITIAL LANDINGS AND NIGHT

DEFENSIVE POSITION

MILES

MT KAGMAN
479

Kagman Peninsula

Laulau

MAGICIENNE

BAY

Afetna Point

MT FINA SUSU
294

Lake Susupe

Charan Kanoa

ASLITO
AIRFIELD

Nafutan Point

Agingan Point

Cape Obiam

RED 2
RED 3

GREEN 1
GREEN 2
GREEN 3

BLUE 1
BLUE 2

YELLOW 1
YELLOW 2
YELLOW 3

ASSAULT ON SAIPAN

June 16-17, 1944

For two days, the Marines assaulted along an irregular front. The 2nd Marines moved north toward Garapan. The 8th east into the swamps near Lake Susupe. And the 6th pushed northeast into Mount Tipo Pali.

It was close combat. No exceptions for battalion commanders. Colonel Chambers, commanding the 3/25 Marines of the 4th Division, described his experiences: "We got to a giant bomb crater. The soil had been all turned up, and around it was three Marines protected by the dirt. I called over to one of these Marines and asked what was going on. He said an antiaircraft gun was right in front of them. I crawled to within two feet of the top of that dirt and raised on my hands to see for myself.

"In less than thirty yards, I was looking into the muzzle of an 88mm antitank gun. The Japs had swung the damn thing around and pointed it right up the hill. I was looking clear down its muzzle. I dropped as hard as I could, and then the damn gun went off. The shell tore through the far side of the bomb crater and came through the dirt near where I was. It took the head off the Marine right next to me. The shell landed and detonated another thirty feet beyond me. Later that same day, we had another close call.

"We advanced and uncovered some Jap supply caches. One was an ammo dump. At 1500, the Japs blew the dump where I was standing and caused many concussion casualties —including myself. I still don't remember a thing about it. Marines told me that when the blast went off, I got thrown right up in the air and turned a complete flip and then landed on my face."

On the night of the 16th, the Japanese launched a major attack against the 6th Marines. This time with forty-four tanks. This battle was a madhouse of noise tracers and flashing lights. As tanks were hit and set on fire, they silhouetted other tanks that came out of flickering shadows to the front. Marines fired in with grenade launchers, 2.36-inch rocket launchers, 75mm self-propelled guns, artillery, and tanks. When it was over and dawn broke, the shattered hulks of twenty-seven Japanese tanks lay there smoking.

In the Susupe swamp, Marines drove inland to the east toward the objective of Aslito Airfield. In danger of overextending his lines. General Holland Smith pulled the 165th Infantry out of reserve and sent them ashore to reinforce the 4th Marine division. On the same day, General Ralph Smith came ashore to command the additional Army 27th Infantry Division units as they landed.

With the 24th Marines on its left flank and the 165th Infantry on its right, the 25th Marines advanced to the north edge of Aslito Airfield late on June 17.

Patrols found the airstrip abandoned, but the 165th (tasked to capture it) waited until the next day. On the same day, June 17, Admiral Spruance made a critical command decision. The formidable main Japanese fleet approached Saipan. He ordered his carriers to meet the enemy ships. That night, he withdrew his supply ships and transports from their offshore positions to a safe distance from the Japanese threat.

June 18, D +3

When the rifleman woke the following day, they looked out in amazement at an empty ocean. Waves of anxious questions must have raced through their minds. Where the hell are our ships? What about our food and ammunition? Will we have the star shell illumination and naval gunfire support? The rifleman in front-line combat had no way of knowing that 33,000 tons of cargo had already been unloaded before the ships withdrew.

That same morning, the 4th Marine Division's attack objective was the seizure of the O-3 line. This meant splitting the Japanese forces in two by reaching the east coast of Saipan. But first, the 23rd Marines had to seize a part of the O-2 line in its zone. This would be the division's line of departure. This meant that the entire division, with its three infantry regiments, the 23rd, 24th, and 25th Marines, jumped off at 1040.

Both the 24th and 25th Marines were able to reach O-3 before dark.

Intense Japanese mortar and machine-gun fire stalled the 23rd Marines. The bombardment came from the east of Lake Susupe on the boundary line separating the two Marine divisions. This made it uncertain which division was responsible for destroying these enemy positions. It was impossible to fire artillery on them for fear of friendly fire. As a result, the 23rd Marines suffered heavy casualties. At days end, a gap still existed between the 2nd and 4th Marine Divisions.

In combat, the bizarre can become routine. One of the 23rd Marines' 75mm half-tracks fired into a Japanese cave. A dense cloud of noxious fumes poured out. A gas alarm sounded. This was serious trouble because the riflemen had long jettisoned the burdensome gas masks. Relief flooded through the men as they established the fumes weren't poisonous and came from picric acid the Japanese stored in the cave.

In the 2nd Division's zone to the north, the 8th Marines

fought bitterly to control Hill 240. A heavily defended coconut grove required saturation fire from the artillery of the 10th Marines before the riflemen could smash their way in and destroy the enemy. By the night of June 18, the two Marine divisions had suffered over five thousand casualties.

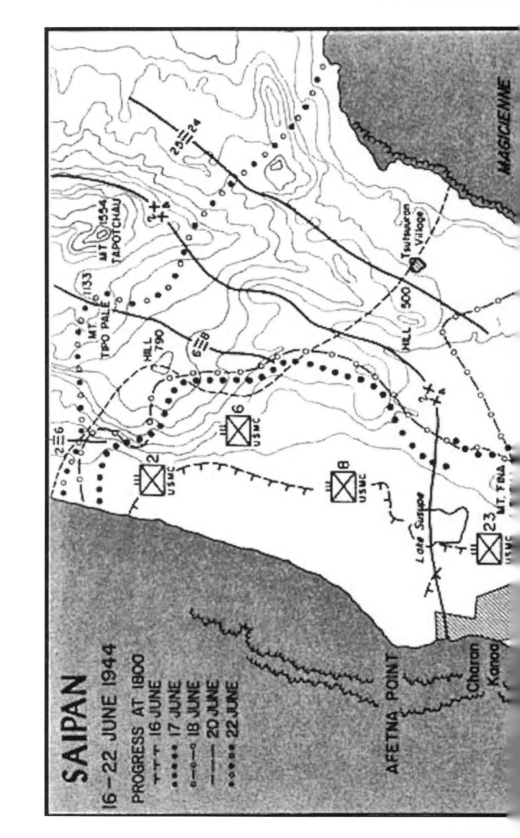

SAIPAN
16–22 JUNE 1944

PROGRESS AT 1800

⊤⊤⊤ 16 JUNE
●●●● 17 JUNE
ᴏ—ᴏ—ᴏ 18 JUNE
———— 20 JUNE
●●●● 22 JUNE

AFETNA POINT

Charan
Kanoa

Lake Susupe

MT. FINA
2 3 USMC

8 USMC

6 USMC

2 USMC

2⹀6

HILL 790

6⹀8

MT. TIPO PALE
1133

MT. 1554
TAPOTCHAU

2⹀4

25⹀24

HILL 500

Tsutsuuran
Village

MAGICIENNE

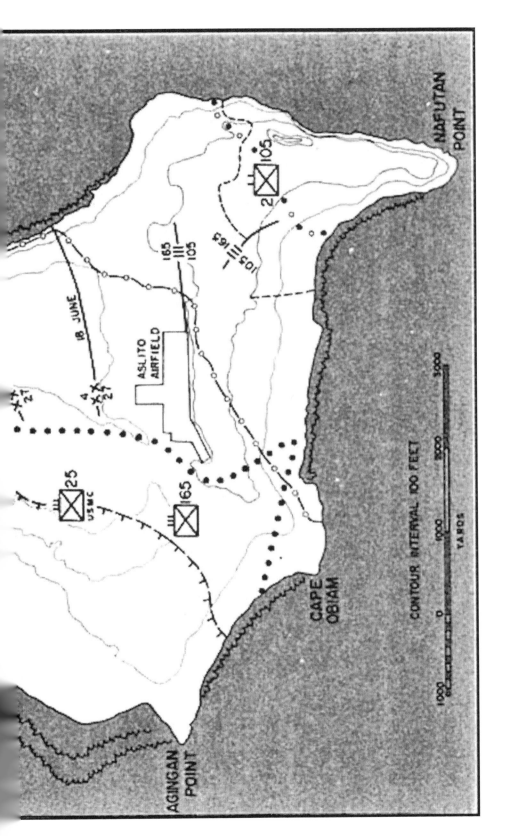

NAFUTAN POINT

AGINGAN POINT

CAPE OBIAM

ASLITO AIRFIELD

18 JUNE

105

2

165
105

105
165

25
USMC

165

4
21

21

CONTOUR INTERVAL 100 FEET

YARDS

0   1000   2000   3000

1000   BEACH LINE FENCES

GREAT MARIANA'S TURKEY SHOOT

June 19-22, 1944

The most significant event of the entire Saipan campaign took place at sea. The two carrier task forces clashed in a colossal air battle. And when it was over, the Japanese suffered a devastating loss of three-hundred and thirty planes out of the four hundred and thirty they'd launched. US Navy flyers called it "The Great Mariana's Turkey Shoot" because of the extreme loss inflicted on the Japanese.

With the help of American submarines and additional carrier plane attacks the next day, the Japanese attempt to relieve Saipan was smashed by a decisive US naval victory. The doom of the enemy garrison was now assured. The American supply ships returned offshore to unload their remaining cargo.

During this time, the 105th Infantry moved slowly along the south coast. They joined the 165th Infantry, sealing off Japanese survivors at Nafutan Point. Once the Japanese were trapped, the 105th were assigned to destroy them. The rest of the 27th Division, including the 165th Infantry, were ordered north as a reserve.

June 19–22 marked a shift in direction for American troops. By pivoting the 2nd Marines onto the far-left flank along the western shore, other Marine regiments swung around from their drive, which had reached the east coast at Magicienne Bay.

On June 20, the 4th Division confronted a key objective. A young lieutenant later recalled: "We had a perfect chance to watch a battalion of the 25th attack. They were in action less than a quarter mile from us. The whole landscape was spread out before us. They assaulted Hill 500, the dominant terrain feature of the entire area. It was obvious they were running into a solid wall of Jap fire. Using artillery timed fire, smoke, and tanks—they stormed to the top and took it. The use of those supporting arms was an overwhelming spectacle. From our vantage point, we watched the timed fire raging in cave entrances and down the face of the hill as if it were going down a stepladder. On lower levels, flamethrower tanks sprouted their napalm Jets upward into other caves. It was quite a show."

In the 2nd Division's area, the 8th Marines wheeled to attack north into the foothills of Mount Tapotchau.

Both Marine divisions now faced serious problems. Their northern drive was stalled by Lieutenant General Yoshitsugu Saitō's main line of defense, running east to west across the island. The terrain into where the attack had to go was a nightmare of caves, hills, valleys, ravines, and cliffs—fortified and defended to the death by Japanese troops.

On June 21, the frontline troops got a reprieve. They rested at their positions, caught up on deeply needed sleep, got some water, and even had a hot meal. They got their first 10-in-1 rations in addition to their K rations.

Intensive preparations were made for a coordinated attack by both Marine divisions the following day. Eighteen artillery battalions were massed for supporting fire. Combat efficiency was rated as satisfactory, despite the sobering total of over six thousand casualties.

On June 22, the Marines attacked all along the line. The 6th Marines overran parts of Mount Tipo Pali, while the 8th Marines worked their way into the maze of gullies and ridges forming Mount Tapotchau's foothills.

On the right flank, the 24th Marines were forced into the messy business of blasting caves along Magicienne Bay. In one of the mortar platoons, a weird encounter took place as described by Lieutenant Joe Cushing: "I bent over one of my mortars and checking the lay of it when I felt a tap on my shoulder, and a guy asked me, 'Hey Mac, are you Marine?' I turned around, and a Jap officer stood less than a foot away from me. I dropped to the ground speechless, and one of my men riddled that Jap from head to toe."

On the left of the 4th Division's area, the 25th Marines advanced 2,400 yards. The forward lines reached an area where the Kagman Peninsula jetted off to the east. This resulted in a substantially increased frontage that the two Marine divisions couldn't cover. To deal with this General Holland Smith ordered his reserve, the Army's 27th Infantry Division to the center of the line and left one battalion of the 105th Infantry in the rear to continue its attempt to eliminate Japanese pockets on the bypassed Nafutan Point.

June 22 marked the arrival of the 19th Fighter Squadron from the US Army Air Forces. P-47 Thunderbolts, launched from Navy escort carriers, landed at Aslito Airfield. The P-47s were fitted with launching racks for rockets by ground crews after they landed. Later that day, eight planes took off in the first support mission of the Saipan campaign. There were only two Marine observation squadrons, VMO-2 and VMO-4, involved in the battle for Saipan. They provided invaluable artillery spotting for the two Marine divisions.

While these developments took place, down in the rock-bottom basic life of infantry platoons, days of relentless combat pressure were embodied by the impact of the regular duties in high-stress levels on the platoon commanders: "I'd made a final inspection of the platoon position and then sacked in—exhausted. When it was my turn to stand watch, it took every reserve of willpower and strength to get up and go on duty. For hours, I alternated between fighting off sleepiness and sweating out the noises and movements that encircled us. I spotted a dark shape, darker than the other shadows. It was the size of a man's head. I watched for a long time, nerves on edge, finger on my M-1 carbine trigger. It moved. I fired a shot. Nothing happened. It would've been suicide to go over and investigate. In the darkness and jungle my men would have shot me in a second. So, when it came time for my relief, I pointed out the suspicious object to the next man and told him to watch closely. Then I collapsed into a dead-tired sleep.

"At dawn, first thing I did was look over where I'd shot the night before. Lying on top of a rock was a gas mask from one of my men. The owner had been sleeping right beside it—a miracle he hadn't been hit."

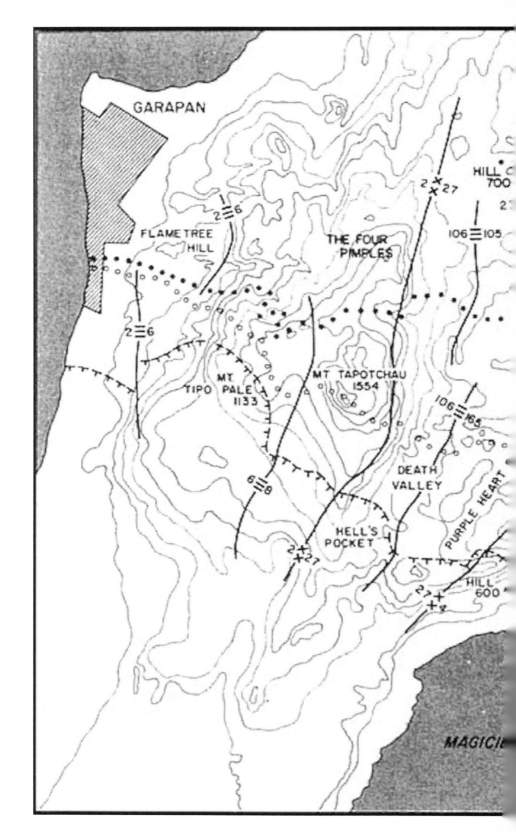

GARAPAN

HILL C 700

2 ╳ 27

106 ≡ 105

21

FLAME TREE HILL

THE FOUR PIMPLES

2 ≡ 6

2 ≡ 6

MT. TIPO PALE 1133

MT TAPOTCHAU 1554

106 ≡ 65

6 ≡ 8

DEATH VALLEY

PURPLE HEART

2 ╳ 27

HELL'S POCKET

27 ╳

HILL 600

MAGICIE

SAIPAN
23–30 JUNE 1944
PROGRESS AT 1800

TTTT 23 JUNE
ooooo 25 JUNE
••••• 30 JUNE

Hashigoru

165 ☰ 23 Donnay

27 +
 + 4

hacha

2 3
|||
2 4

KAGMAN
PENINSULA

MT KAGMAN
400

CONTOUR INTERVAL 100 FEET

0   1000   2000   3000   4000
YARDS

MARINES STORM GARAPAN

July 1-4, 1944

General Holland Smith turned his attention to the operational plans for driving through the northern third of Saipan. He intended to bring the campaign to a successful, even if bloody, finish. His next objective ran eastward across the island to Tanapag and then up Garapan on the west coast. The 2nd Marine Division would be held in reserve near Flores Point.

This left the 4th Marine Division and the 27th Infantry Division ready to attack General Saitō's troops and defenses. The *easiest* assignment during this period fell on the shoulders of the 4th Marine Division on the east coast. They advanced over three thousand yards against light opposition, veering left and ending on July 4 with their left flank less than two-thousand yards north of Tanapag.

What seemed like light opposition to General Schmidt in his divisional command post looked quite different to a tired lieutenant who described a typical rifle platoon on the morning of July 1: "I took the rest of my men, and we cautiously combed the area. It was a terrible place. Rocks and creepers were so interwoven that they formed an impenetrable barrier. Visibility was limited to only a few feet. After my sergeant was wounded, the atmosphere of the place became even more tense.

"We found some rock crevices that the Japs might be hiding in. I tried calling to them in our Japanese combat phrases to come out and surrender. This proved fruitless. The Japs knew exactly where we were. I had no idea where they were. I tried to maneuver a flamethrower man into a position where he could give the crevice a blast without becoming a target. But because of the ground's composition, this proved impossible.

"It was then we heard a shot off to our left. We headed over to investigate and then all hell broke loose. An automatic Jap weapon opened to our left. We all hit the deck. No one was hit (for a change). But we couldn't locate the weapon. I called to the man over on the left flank. No answer. What happened?

"More enemy fire spattered our small group of Marines. The source was right on top of us. I told two of my men to throw grenades at the area they thought the fire was coming from—twenty feet away. Under that cover, we worked a rifleman forward a couple yards to get a bead on that Jap, but he couldn't spot him, and the enemy fire grew heavier.

"Here we were—isolated from the rest of the company with only six of us left—our flank man had disappeared. We took heavy fire from an uncertain number of Japs we couldn't locate right in our middle. Some men were getting jittery, so I tried to be as calm and cool as I could, although I didn't feel that way on the inside. I moved back to the other end of the hilltop and reported to our company commander on the phone. If I could get his okay, I would then [contact another one of our platoons] for reinforcements, and we could move back into this area and clear out the Jap pocket.

"Our relentless advance against the Jap defenses would often result in face-to-face encounters. After three days, I saw another remarkable act of bravery: Three of our tanks came down the road. They turned to the south, which took them off the high ground and into a cave with literally hundreds of Japs, swarming all over our tanks. We watched and heard the lieutenant who commanded them screaming for help on the radio—and I don't blame him. They formed a triangle and covered each other as best as they could."

The commanding officer closest to the crisis was Lieutenant Colonel Hollis "Musty" Mustain, in charge of the 1/25 Marines. He recalled the incident later: "My executive officer was a regular major named Fenton Mee. We were together and when the radio operators told us what was happening. I turned to Mee and said, 'Get some people in and get those damn tanks out.' Major Mee turned to his battalion CP (all staff people) and said, 'Let's get going.' Then he turned and took off. I can still see his face like it was yesterday—he must've figured he was going to get killed. But they got there, and the Japs pulled out. This saved our tanks. It was one of the bravest things I ever saw anyone do."

By July 4, only six officers remained out of twenty-eight, and three-hundred enlisted men out of the six hundred and ninety remained in those companies. Including the headquarters company, only 468 men remained in the battalion's original strength of over 1,050. One rifle company had to be disbanded. Another battalion repeated this macabre toll with twenty-two officers killed out of twenty-nine and four hundred and ninety enlisted men killed or wounded in action.

The 27th Infantry Division advanced in the center of the line of attack. They had a far easier time than in the grinding experience they had previously come through. Their advance also veered left and against "negligible resistance" with the enemy in full flight.

The 2nd Marines stormed into Garapan and seized Flametree Hill. The regiment found the town in shambles.

The town had been leveled by Marine artillery and naval gunfire. Twisted metal rooftops covered the area, shielding Japanese snipers. Several deftly hidden pillboxes were spread among the ruins. Engineers, covered by riflemen, slid behind obstacles, and set up explosives while flamethrowers seared the front. With the help of tanks and 75mm self-propelled guns, the 2nd Marines eliminated the scattered resistance before nightfall.

On the beaches, suppressing fire from the LVT(A)s of the 2nd Armored Amphibian Battalion destroyed Japanese weapons near the water. The 2nd Marines moved past the town into Flores Point, halfway to Tanapag. Their uniforms were filthy. Stiff with sweat and dirt from two weeks of fierce fighting. Marines gleefully dipped their heads into the cool ocean water.

The other two divisions had veered their attack to the left and already reached the northwest coast. The 2nd Marine Division went into reserve as planned on July 4. General Holland Smith anticipated the end in sight for Saipan. He wanted to rest the 2nd Division and use them for the next assault on neighboring Tinian Island.

The Japanese withdrew to a defensive line north of Garapan. The American attack not only shattered their manpower, artillery, and tanks, but the enemy was desperate for food. Many starving Japanese troops turned to eating field grass and tree bark.

TENNO HAIKA! BANZAI

July 5-8, 1944

The Japanese retreat left many of their men behind in caves to fight to the death. This tactic posed to American troops the life-threatening question of whether the civilians hidden inside should be saved.

First Lieutenant Fred Stott of the 1/24 Marines wrote of his experiences: "It was the twenty first day of the battle, and we trudged along a winding trail to relieve the 23rd Marines for an attack scheduled at 1300. A typical artillery barrage followed by *morale-lifting* rockets was unleashed against cave-dwelling Japs. But neither was effective. The Japs used civilian men, women, and children as decoys. The cost was heavy. Jap soldiers dressed as civilian prisoners succeeded in killing a dozen men from A Company."

This kind of treacherous warfare continued.

The next day 1st Lieutenant Stott described how he dealt with the Japanese deception: "A few Japs played possum by smearing the blood of other dead Japs on themselves and lying still as the Marines walked up. I gave my Marines instructions to 'stick it if it didn't stink.' Marines had the grim duty of bayoneting all the bodies.

"We also picked up civilian prisoners, including women and children. Marines took some serious risks. They went into caves, not knowing whether there were soldiers hiding inside, in order to rescue civilians. The minute they got civilians out, they fed them with part of their rations and offered the men cigarettes."

After the 2nd Division was put into reserve, it was clear to General Holland Smith that a banzai attack would come. He warned all units to be alert and paid a personal visit on July 6 to General Griner, now in command of the 27th Infantry Division. He stressed the likelihood of an attack coming down the coastline onto the flat ground of Tanapag Plain.

General Holland Smith had been furious with General

Ralph Smith, and after discussing the matter with Admiral-Turner, he relieved Ralph Smith of command of the 27th Infantry Division on June 24 and sent him to Hawaii. By the Morning of the 25th he was temporarily replaced by Major General Jaraman, who was then replaced by Major General Griner on the June 28th. This conflict created a grudge between the Marines and the Army "that lasted well after the war."

While General Holland Smith had the authority to do this, many said it was a rash decision and that he hadn't considered the challenging terrain the 27th Division faced on Saipan. A report on an interview with General Holland Smith paraphrased him explaining that his decision was for the best because, under Ralph Smith, men were being wasted and more were dying than necessary, and they hadn't even accomplished their objective while the two Marine divisions had moved forward.

While General Holland Smith was preparing his men for a banzai attack, General Saitō and his Japanese troops were cornered in his sixth and last command post. It was a miserable cave north of Tanapag in the Paradise Valley. This valley was pounded by naval gunfire and artillery. Saitō only had fragments of his troops left. He was sick, hungry, and wounded. Saitō gave orders for one final and fanatical banzai charge while he committed *hara-kiri* in his cave.

On July 6 at 1000, he faced east and shouted: "Tenno Haika! Banzai" (Long live the Empire for ten-thousand ages). He drew his blood first with his sword and then his assistant shot him and Admiral Chūichi Nagumo in the back of the head with a pistol. But not before he ordered the commencement of the final attack at 0300 on July 7 and said [translated], "Whether we attack or whether we stay where we are, there is only death."

Another all-out enemy charge was nothing new to the Marines and soldiers on Saipan. One rifleman recounted his experiences: "Whenever we cornered the Japs, and there was no way out, we faced that damn banzai attack. The 23rd Marines had fought off a few of these on our Saipan adventures. I dreaded these attacks but also welcomed them. While they created a great deal of fear, when it was finally over, that sector was Jap-free.

"For hours, we heard them preparing for a banzai attack. It was their end, and they knew it. They wouldn't surrender. It was against their training and heritage. All that was left was one last charge of pouring all their troops into one concentrated place—trying to kill as many of us as they could."

The rifleman's account continued with dramatic descriptions of the stressful waiting he endured while listening to enemy shouts and screams going on for hours. The noise increased as Marine mortars and artillery hammered toward the shouting—adding to the deafening din. Marines waited in foxholes with clips of ammo placed close so they could reload fast. They fixed bayonets to their rifles—ensured knives were loose in their scabbards. They waited in jittery anticipation of the imminent attacks.

Listening to the screams, their senses were alert and finely tuned. But there was a silence. A silence that signaled the enemy's advance. Then: "What sounded like a thousand people screaming all at once. A horde of madmen broke out of the darkness. Screams of 'banzai' choked the air—Japanese officers led these 'devils from hell' with their swords drawn and swishing in circles over their heads. Japanese soldiers followed their officers, firing their weapons and screaming 'banzai' as they charged.

"Our weapons opened up. Mortars and machine guns fired like gangbusters. They didn't fire in bursts of three or five, but belt after belt of ammo went through the gun. The gunner swiveled the barrel to the left and right. Jap bodies mounted up in front of us, but they still charged, running over their comrades' fallen bodies. Mortar tubes and machine gun barrels got so hot from the rapid-fire—they could no longer be used.

"While each attack had taken its toll, they still came in droves. To this day, I can even now visualize the enemy only a few feet away—bayonets aimed at us as we emptied clip after clip into them. Their momentum carried them into our foxholes, right on top of us. Then, after pushing the dead Jap body off me, I'd reload and do it all over again.

"Deafening screams, bullets whizzing around us, the reek of death and smell of Japanese gunpowder permeated the air. I was full of fear and hate and the desire to kill. I believed the Japanese were a savage animal, a devil, a beast, not human. The only thought I had was to kill, kill, kill—until finally, it ended."

That was the mayhem General Holland Smith predicted as the final spastic effort of the Japanese. And it came in the early morning hours of July 7. The pivotal moment in the Battle for Saipan. The Japanese tactical objective was to smash through Garapan and Tanapag, reaching down to Charan-

Kanoa. It was a fearful charge of fire and flesh, primitive and savage. Some of the Japanese troops were only armed with rocks or with a knife mounted on a pole.

This banzai charge also hit the 105th Infantry dug in for the night on the main line of resistance. With the regimental headquarters directly behind them, the 105th left a five-hundred-yard gap between them which they planned to cover by fire. The Japanese found this gap, poured through, and headed pell-mell for the regimental headquarters. The men of the frontline battalions fought bravely but failed to stop the banzai onslaught.

Behind the 105th were three artillery battalions of the 10th Marines. The gunners couldn't set their fuses fast enough, even when cut down to five-tenths of a second, to stop the Japanese enemy on top of them. They lowered their muzzles of their 105mm howitzers and spewed ricochet fire by bouncing shells off the ground. Many of their other guns couldn't fire at all because the Army troops ahead of them mixed in with the Japanese attackers.

Marines in the artillery battalions fired every type of small weapon they could. One of their battalions was almost wiped out when the battalion commander was killed. The cane fields to the front swarmed with enemy troops. Guns were overrun, and Marine artillerymen, after removing their guns' firing locks, fell back and joined the fight as infantry.

As the firestorm broke on the 105th, men of the nearby 165th Infantry were ordered "to stand where they were and shoot Japs" without moving forward. By 1600 that afternoon, after coming to the aid of the shattered 105th, the 165th was still three hundred yards short of making contact.

Savage hand-to-hand fighting took the momentum out of the Japanese surge. They were finally stopped by the 105th, less than eight hundred yards south of Tanapag. By 1800, the lost ground had been regained.

A shocking day of casualties. The 105th Infantry's two battalions took 917 casualties while killing 2,291 Japanese. One Marine artillery battalion had 127 casualties but had accounted for 322 of the enemy. The final count of the Japanese dead reached a staggering total of 4,321, some due to shell fire, but the vast majority were killed in the banzai charge.

During the bloodshed, there were countless acts of bravery. Recognized and later awarded the Army Medal of Honor for leadership and "resistance to the death" were Army Colonel William O'Brien, commanding a battalion of the 105th, and one of his squad leaders, Sergeant Tom Baker.

While most attention was centered on the bloody coastal battle, the 23rd Marines attacked a strong Japanese force well protected by caves in an inland cliff. The key to eliminating them was truck-mounted rocket launchers, lowered over the cliff by chains attached to tanks. Once lowered to the base, their fire, supplemented by offshore rocket gunboats, snuffed out the remaining enemy resistance.

The next day on July 8, saw the beginning of the end. The Japanese spent the last of their manpower on banzai charges. It was now time for the final American mop-up. LVTs rescued men of the 105th Infantry who'd waded out from the shore to the reef to escape the Japanese. General Holland Smith placed most of the 27th Infantry Division back into reserve. He then put the 2nd Marine Division back in the line of attack with the 105th Infantry attached. Together with the 4th Marine Division, they swept north toward the end of the island.

Along the coast was a bizarre spectacle that presented a macabre end to the campaign: Japanese troops in the area had destroyed themselves with suicidal rushes from the high cliffs to the rocky beach below. Japanese troops were observed, along with hundreds of civilians, wading out to sea and drowning themselves. Some troops committed hara-kiri with knives or destroyed themselves with grenades. Some officers even used their swords to decapitate their troops.

UNBELIEVABLE SELF DESTRUCTION

July 9, 1944

It was to be the final day of a brutal campaign. The 4th Marines reached Marpi Point on the northern end of the island, while the 6th and 8th Marines came down from the hills to occupy the last western beaches.

Colonel Chambers watched as this grim scene played out: "We moved along the cliffs and caves, uncovering civilians along the way. Japanese soldiers refused to surrender and would not allow civilians to surrender. I watched as women, some carrying children, stumbled out of the caves toward our lines. They were shot down by Japanese troops in the back. I watched more women carrying children come out to the cliffs that dropped to the ocean.

"These were steep cliffs. Some women came down and threw their children into the ocean and jumped after them to commit suicide. I watched one group of about nine civilian men, women, and children get into a little huddle and blow themselves up. It was the saddest and most terrible thing I've ever seen, and yet I presume quite consistent with the Japanese code of Bushido."

Another lieutenant from the same division witnessed other unbelievable forms of self-destruction: "The interpreters were summoned, and they begged using an amplifier for civilians to come forward and surrender. No movement at first. Then people came closer into a compact mass. It seemed to be predominantly civilians, but several uniforms could be seen circling about in the throng—using the civilians for protection.

"As they huddled closer, I heard a weird singing chant. Then a Rising Sun flag unfurled. Movement grew more agitated. Men leaped into the sea. The chanting gave way to startled cries and then that popping sound of detonating grenades. It was a handful of soldiers determined to prevent the surrender or escape of the civilians by tossing grenades into the throng of men, women, and children. Then the Japs dived into the sea, from which escape was impossible. Exploding grenades shattered the mob into pieces of wounded and dying. It was the first time I actually saw water that ran red with human blood."

This kind of fanaticism characterized the Japanese. Not surprising that over 23,800 of the enemy were known dead—with uncounted thousands of others charred by flamethrowers and sealed forever in caves. Only 736 prisoners of war were taken, and of these 430 were Koreans. American casualties numbered 16,612.

On July 9 at 1615, Saipan was declared secured (although mopping up continued for long after). The 4th Marine division was later awarded the Presidential Unit Citation for their outstanding combat performance on Saipan and later assault on the neighboring island of Tinian.

LEGACY OF SAIPAN

The fighting on Saipan not only caused many American casualties but foreshadowed the bloody fighting that lay ahead in the western and central Pacific. General Holland Smith called it, "the decisive battle for the Pacific offensive and opening the way to the home islands."

Japanese General Saitō wrote: "The fate of the Empire would be decided in this one action." Another Japanese admiral had agreed, "Our war was lost with the loss of Saipan." This was a truly strategic strike for victory in the Pacific War.

The proof of these vital decisions was demonstrated four months later when one-hundred B-29 bombers took off from Saipan bound for Tokyo. There were other significant results. The US had secured an advanced naval base to deliver punishing strikes close to enemy shores. Emperor Hirohito was forced to consider a diplomatic settlement of war. General Tojo, the premier, and his entire cabinet fell from power on July 18—nine days after losing Saipan.

The lessons learned in this grisly campaign would be

applied to future amphibious operations. Flaws would be analyzed and corrected. The clear need to improve aviation support for ground troops led to better results in the Philippine Islands and Okinawa and Iwo Jima. Artillery spotting missions flown by the Marine Observation Squadron (VMO-2 and -4) set a pattern for the use of light planes in the future.

Naval gunfire support was also closely reviewed. General Saitō wrote, "If there were no naval gunfire, we could have fought it out with the enemy in a decisive battle." But over 8,500 tons of ammunition were fired by US Navy ships. The trajectory of the flat naval guns proved somewhat limiting, as the shells didn't have the penetrating and plunging effect needed against Japanese strongholds.

Lessons learned from the supply confusion that marred the early days on the beaches had improved little since the days of the Guadalcanal landing. The logistic problems arose because: once a beach was in friendly hands, ships unloaded as quickly as possible and sailors in the landing craft hurried to get into the beaches and back out again. Supplies were spread all over the beach, partly because of the enemy's artillery and mortar harassing fire on the beaches but also because of the Marine Corps' hard-driving rapid attack.

Estimates of resupply requirements were way too small. For example, a shortage of radio batteries was never corrected. There was insufficient time to sort and separate equipment and supplies adequately. This caused mix-ups with Marine uniforms getting into Army dumps, an Army supply showing up at Marine dumps.

After the beach chaos at Saipan, the Navy decided to organize a permanent shore party for the future. It would be responsible for the movement of all supplies from the beach to the dumps and then the later issue to the divisions.

The tactical lessons learned were also new to the Pacific

war. Instead of assaulting a small atoll, the fighting had been one of movement on a sizable landmass, further complicated by a maze of caves and Japanese defensive systems. The enemy had defended caves before, but never on such a huge scale. On Saipan, these caves were both man-made and natural. Often, the vegetation gave them excellent camouflage. Some caves had steel doors which could be opened for an artillery piece or machine gun to fire and then withdraw before return fire could destroy them. Flame-throwing tanks proved useful in reaching these caves, but the range was limited on Saipan. This was improved for future operations.

The challenging experiences on Saipan led to a variety of changes that saved American lives in future Pacific campaigns. Losing the island was a strategic strike from which the Japanese would never recover—while the United States pressed forward to ultimate victory.

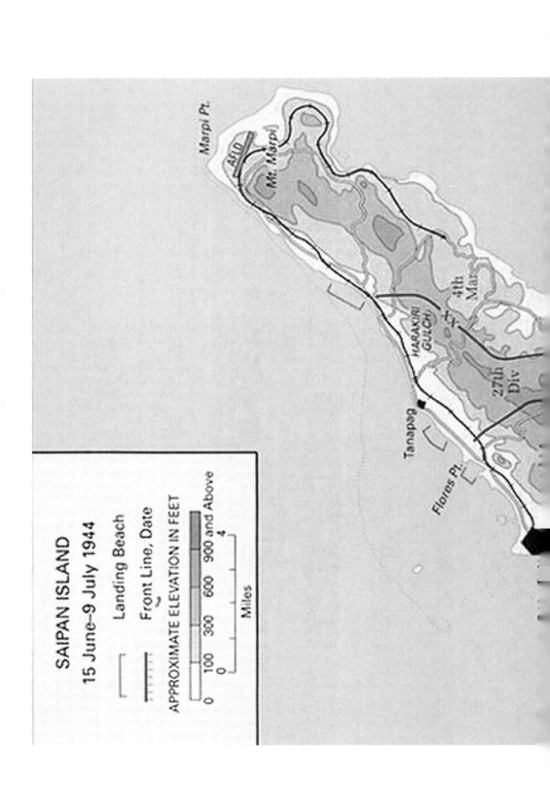

SAIPAN ISLAND
15 June–9 July 1944

Landing Beach
Front Line, Date

APPROXIMATE ELEVATION IN FEET

0   100   300   600   900 and Above

Miles
0   4

Marpi Pt.

A510

Mt. Marpi

Tanapag

Flores Pt.

HARAKIRI
GULCH

4th
Mar

27th
Div

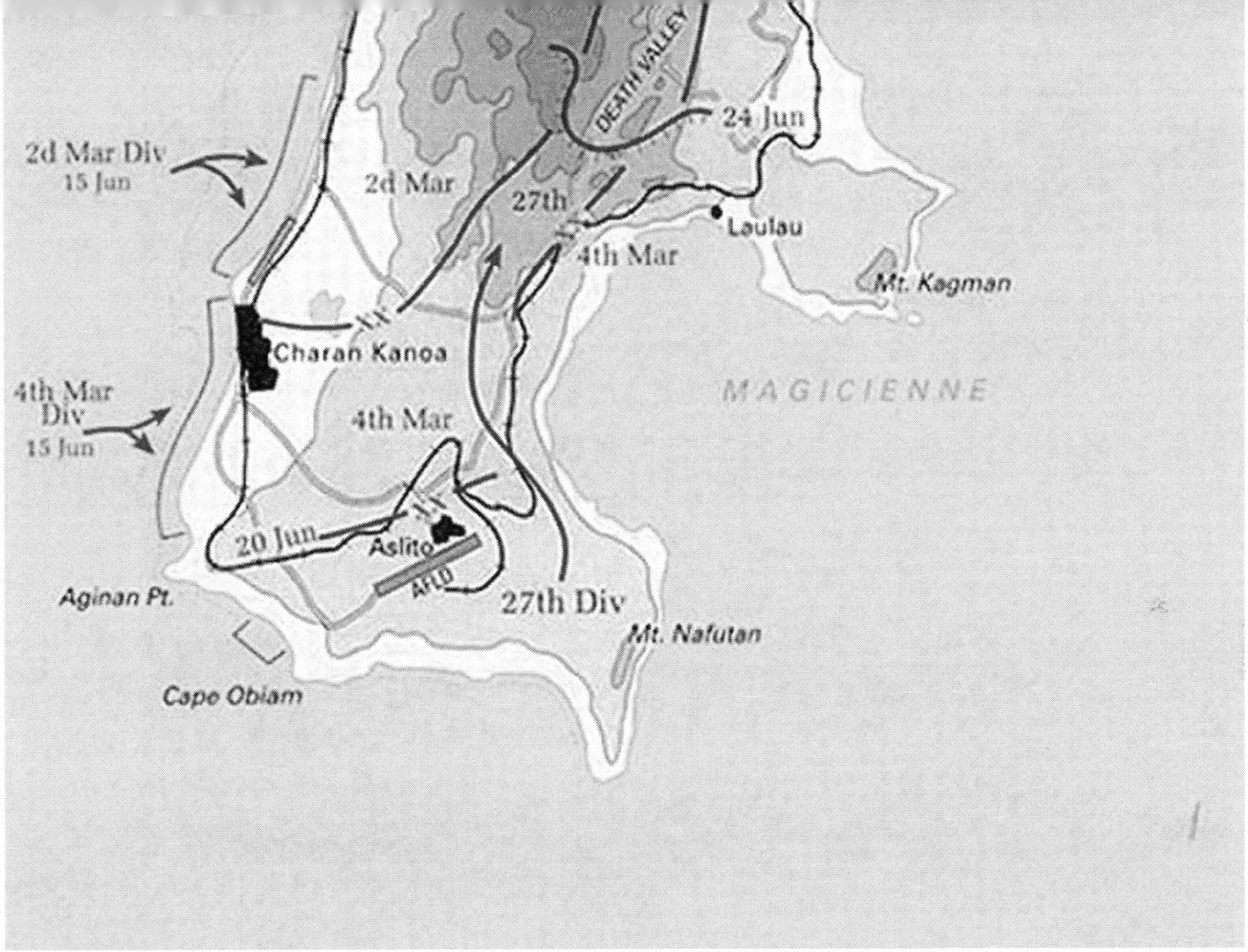

MAGICIENNE

Mt. Kagman

Laulau

DEATH VALLEY

24 Jun

4th Mar

27th

2d Mar

Mt. Nafutan

27th Div

Charan Kanoa

4th Mar

Aslito AFD

20 Jun

2d Mar Div
15 Jun

4th Mar
Div
15 Jun

Agingan Pt.

Cape Obiam

GENERAL HOLLAND M. SMITH

Born in 1882, General Holland Smith became one of the most famous Marines of World War II. He was commissioned as a 2nd lieutenant in 1905 and assigned overseas. He served in Nicaragua, Santo Domingo, Philippines and with the Marine brigade in France in World War I.

In the early 1930s, he concentrated on developing amphibious warfare strategy and tactics. Soon after the outbreak of war with Japan in 1941, he received a key position —command of all Marines in the Central Pacific.

Described by a fellow Marine officer as, "medium height, maybe five feet nine and somewhat paunchy. His once black hair is now gray. His once close-trimmed mustache, scraggly. He wore steel-rimmed glasses and smoked cigars ceaselessly."

He had one other feature that characterized him: a temper so fierce that he earned the nickname "Howling Mad" Smith —his close friends knew him as Hoke

His fierce temper would usually emerge as irritation at what he felt were inadequate performances. One famous example was his relief of Army General Ralph Smith on Saipan. A huge inter-service uproar ensued.

After his 41 years of active service, he was awarded four Distinguished Service Medals for his leadership in four successful amphibious operations. He retired in April 1946, as a four-star general. General Smith died in 1967 at a US Naval Hospital in San Diego. He was 84 years old.

GENERAL HARRY SCHMIDT

General Schmidt was born in 1886 and entered the Marine Corps as a 2nd lieutenant in 1909. By an extraordinary coincidence, his first foreign duty was in Guam in the Mariana Islands—where he would return thirty-three years later under vastly different circumstances. He led the 4th Marine Division on the assaults in the Marshall Islands at Roi-Namur, and then onto Saipan in the Marianas.

He served in Mexico, Philippines, Cuba, and Nicaragua (where he was awarded a Navy Cross, second only to the Medal of Honor). Combined with repeated stays in China, it was a truly diverse overseas career. A fellow Marine officer described him as, "a Buddha, a typical old-timer Marine. He was regulation, he'd been to China, an old establishment regular Marine."

At the end of World War II, he was decorated with three Distinguished Service Medals. He retired in 1948 after nearly 40 years of service as a four-star general. General Schmidt died on February 10, 1968 and is buried in Fort Rosecrans National Cemetery in San Diego.

GENERAL THOMAS WATSON

General Watson was born in 1892 and began his military career in 1912. He was a fully qualified member of "the Old Corps." After his commission in 1916, he served in a variety of Marine assignments in China, the Caribbean, and the United States.

A brigadier general and commander of Tactical Group-1 built on the 22nd Marines, he led his men in the conquest of Eniwetok Atoll in the Marshall Islands in February 1944. He earned a Distinguished Service Medal and his 22nd Marines were awarded a Navy Unit Commendation.

In April 1944 he took command of the 2nd Marine Division. In June he directed his men in the conquest of Saipan and then the Tinian Islands, receiving his second Distinguished Service Medal.

He had the nickname, "Terrible Tommy." Watson's impatience is depicted by fellow General Wallace Greene: "He wouldn't tolerate for one minute laziness, stupidity, incompetence, or any failure in leadership. His temper and correcting these failings would be fiery," as both Army and Marine officers learned at Eniwetok and Saipan.

He retired in 1950 and passed away in March 1966 as a lieutenant general.

NAVY LIEUTENANT JOHN CRAVEN

The two types of noncombatants attached to Marine units were the Navy Chaplain Corps and Navy Medical Corps. When Marines were in combat, they were well attended to in body and soul on the front lines.

Navy Lieutenant John Craven of the Chaplain Corps earned a Bronze Star for his actions under fire on Saipan. He later wrote: "In combat we were to go from place to place, unit to unit, starting out early in the morning and going until dark. We'd just visit one unit after another and have a brief service. We had some Testaments and small hymn books I could carry in my map case. We'd gather a few men together in a bomb crater, and I would have one service after the other. There were times we had fourteen of those in one day—especially on Sunday.

"We took turns at the cemetery. Each chaplain from different units would go down and take his turn for burials. We had a brief committal service for each man as they brought the bodies in. I tried to keep up with all the men in our units. Where they were if they were in the hospital. I worked closely with the sergeant major, and it was amazing how we could keep up with these men. Especially how and when they were killed and where they were buried."

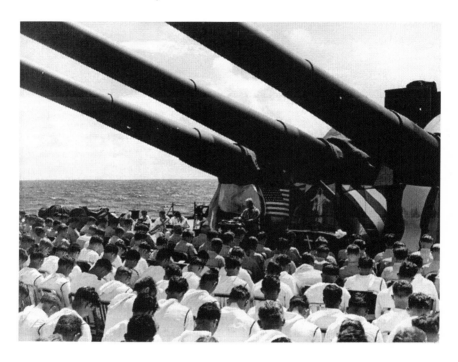

Lieutenant Craven kept a notebook which listed all the casualties. He kept that notebook current day-to-day. At night he'd compare notes with the regiment sergeant major. It helped all the chaplains to know who and where the casualties were. These casualty reports were also some help to the sergeant major because it would verify the reports that he got.

When Chaplain Craven and other chaplains returned to the rear areas of their units, they'd write letters to the families of everyone killed in the regiment and added their letters to those of the commanding officers.

Chaplain Craven used a special type of ministration. He had a canvas gas mask carrier slung over each shoulder. In one carrier he had Scotch whiskey and the other was filled with fried chicken. As he knelt by each young, frightened, and wounded Marine, he'd usually get asked, "Am I going to be okay?"

Chaplain Craven would always answer, "You sure will be," as cheerfully as he could muster. He'd then ask the wounded Marine if he'd like a wing or a drumstick. The young Marine would be so surprised he'd forget about his present circumstances. Then Chaplain Craven would ask if he wanted to wash it down with a swig of Scotch. Most Marines couldn't believe what they were hearing with the hell of confusion, noise, and death surrounding them.

A young doctor tending to the Marine wounded on Saipan later wrote: "Lieutenant Craven probably saved more young lives from dying of shock than will ever be known."

2ND MARINE DIVISION

This division was activated as part of the 2nd Marine Brigade in part of the Fleet Marine Force on July 1,1936. A year later the brigade deployed to Shanghai, China and then returned in 1938 to San Diego, California.

On February 1, 1941, this unit was re-designated as the 2nd Marine Division. The component regiments were the 2nd, 6th, 8th, and 10th Marines. They brought with them impressive histories of service from Mexico (Veracruz), World War I in France, and the Caribbean.

Elements of the division served in Hawaii during the Pearl Harbor attack. Then onto Samoa, before the full division was sent to the Guadalcanal campaign. They continued to the bloody battle on Tarawa, where they were awarded the Presidential Unit Citation before continuing to Saipan, Tinan, and ultimately Okinawa.

The 2nd Marine Division Patch

Marines from the 2nd Division wore this patch on Saipan. It was designed and approved in November 1943. It has the USMC official colors of scarlet and gold. The insignia has a spearhead shaped scarlet background with a hand holding a lit golden torch. The numeral 2 is superimposed in scarlet on the torch and the hand is encircled by five white stars arranged as the Southern Cross constellation. It was under this that the division's first Pacific War combat took place at Guadalcanal.

4TH MARINE DIVISION

This Marine division was born from the shifting and redesignation of several other units. The 23rd Marines began as an infantry detached from the 3rd Division in February 1943. At the same time an artillery battalion became the genesis of the 14th Marines and engineer elements  of the 19th Marines formed the start of the 20th Marines. In March '43, the 24th Marines were organized and then two months later were split to supply men from the 25th Marines.

The wartime shuffling provided the major building blocks for a new division. The units were separated between artillery, medical, transport, weapons, tanks, etc. Some were in Camp Lejeune, North Carolina and had to be moved to Camp Pendleton, San Diego by train and by ship through the Panama Canal in summer of 1943. When all the units were finally together, they formed the 4th Marine Division activated on August 14, 1943.

After intensive training, they shipped out on January 13, 1944, and in less than thirteen months made four major assault landings: Roi-Namur, Saipan, Tinian, and Iwo Jima. The 4th Marine Division suffered over seventeen thousand casualties. They were awarded two Presidential Unit Citations and a Navy Unit Commendation before their deactivation on November 28, 1945. In February 1966 they were reactivated as the lead division in the Marine Corps reserve. The 4th Marine Division also supplied essential units to Desert Storm in the liberation of Kuwait.

Fourth Marine Division Patch

Also worn on Saipan, this patch was designed by Staff Sergeant John Fabiano, a member of the division's public affairs office. His commanding officer was shocked to find that when the division attacked Kwajalein Atoll in the Marshall Islands, the layout of the Japanese airstrips was an exact replica.

ARMY 27TH INFANTRY DIVISION

Before a national emergency was declared in 1940, the Army's 27th Infantry Division served as a New York State National Guard. Composed of several famous old regiments, some even dating to the Revolutionary and Civil wars.

In World War II this division's 165th Infantry had been the legendary old 69th New York Infantry, the "Fighting Irish" of World War I. The first unit of this regiment was organized in 1775.

While the war in Europe intensified, the Selective Service Act gave the president the power to federalize the National Guard. FDR activated the 27th Division on September 25, 1940. They were sent first to Fort McClellan, Alabama for rigorous training and then onto California in December 1941.

On February 28, 1942, the first elements of the 27th Infantry Division sailed from San Francisco and landed in the town of Hilo on Hawaii's "Big Island." For the next two months, the units were scattered throughout the islands for local defense and training. This was the start of the longest wartime overseas service of any National Guard Division in the United States Army.

In the fall of 1942, the division was directed to assemble on the island of Oahu under command of General Ralph Smith. In summer of 1943, orders came in to prepare the 165th Infantry Regiment (reinforced by a battalion of the 105th, and an artillery battalion) to assault and capture the Makin Atoll in the Gilbert Island chain.

After a four-day battle in November 1943, the division supplied a battalion of the 106th Infantry for an unopposed occupation of Majuro in the Marshall Islands in January 1944.

The lead up to Saipan for units of the 27th came the following month. Two battalions of the 106th at Eniwetok Atoll in the Marshals. After the battle on Saipan, they went on to the fight for Okinawa in April 1945, and ultimately to the occupation of Japan in September 1945.

In December 1946, the 27th Infantry division was deactivated.

HEROES OF SAIPAN

Private First Class Harold Agerholm was born on January 29, 1925, in Racine, Wisconsin. He served in the 4th Battalion, 10th Marines in the 2nd Marine Division against enemy Japanese forces on Tarawa Atoll in '43 and on Saipan in '44. It was there that he met his death on July 7, 1944.

The Japanese enemy launched a fierce counterattack and overran a neighboring artillery battalion. Private First Class Agerholm volunteered to check on the hostile attack and help to evacuate the wounded. He located and seized an abandoned ambulance and repeatedly made extremely dangerous trips under heavy small arms and mortar fire. Private First Class Agerholm single-handedly loaded and evacuated over forty wounded men. He worked tirelessly and with utter disregard for his own safety during a grueling period of three hours.

Through intense and persistent enemy fire, he ran out to aid a man whom he believed was a wounded Marine, but in the process was mortally wounded by a Japanese sniper. Private First Class Agerholm was awarded the Medal of Honor posthumously for his brilliant initiative, great personal valor, and self-sacrificing efforts in the face of certain death. His gallantry reflected the highest credit upon himself and the United States.

Private First Class Harold Glenn Epperson was born on July 14, 1923 in Akron, Ohio. He joined the Marines in 1942 and served with the 1st Battalion, 6th Marines in the 2nd Marine Division fighting against Japanese forces on Tarawa Atoll and died on the island of Saipan July 25, 1944.

Private First Class Epperson's machine gun emplacement bore the full brunt of a fanatic enemy assault under the cover of a predawn darkness. Private First Class Epperson manned his weapon with a determined aggressiveness and fought furiously in defense of his battalion's position. He maintained a steady stream of devastating fire against rapidly infiltrating Japanese troops. He aided in breaking that attack up.

A Japanese soldier assumed to be dead sprang up and hurled a hand grenade into the emplacement. Private First Class Epperson, determined to save his comrades, without hesitation sacrificed himself and dove onto the grenade. He absorbed the shattering violence of the exploding charge with his own body. Resolute and stouthearted in the face of certain death, Private First Class Epperson fearlessly yielded his own life to save his comrades. He was awarded the Medal of Honor for his superb valor and unfaltering devotion to duty. His actions reflect the highest credit upon himself and the United States.

Sergeant Grant Timmerman was born on February 14, 1919, in Americus, Kansas. During WWII he served with the 2nd Tank Battalion, 6th Marines in the 2nd Marine Division on Tarawa Atoll and on Saipan. He gave his life in order to save his crew on July 8, 1944.

Sergeant Timmerman advanced with his tank a few yards ahead of the infantry to support a vigorous attack on hostile positions. Sergeant Timmerman maintained a steady fire from his antiaircraft sky mount machine gun until progress was impeded by a series of enemy pillboxes and trenches. He observed a target of opportunity and immediately ordered that the tanks stop.

Mindful of the danger from the muzzle blast, he prepared to open fire with the 75mm. He fearlessly stood up, exposing himself, and ordered the infantry to hit the deck. A grenade hurled by the Japanese was about to drop into the open turret hatch. Sergeant Timmerman blocked the opening with his body allowing the grenade to detonated against his chest, taking the brunt of the explosion.

For his exceptional valor and loyalty in saving his men at the cost of his own life. Sergeant Timmerman, too, was awarded the Medal of Honor.

Building a relationship with my readers is one of the best things about writing. I occasionally send out emails with details on new releases and special offers. If you'd like to join my free readers group and never miss a new release, just go to daniel-wrinn.com and you can sign up for the list.

REFERENCES

Information available for researching the World War II Pacific Theater is vast. I've listed my main reference sources below. Websites, newspaper articles, and even History Channel documentaries also contributed to my research.

Chapin, Captain John C. "Breaching the Marianas - United States Marine Corps." U.S. Marine Corps Reserve (RET), 1994.

Chen, C. Peter. "Mariana Islands Campaign and the Great Turkey Shoot." World War II Database. Lava Development, LLC, 2004.

Chen, C. Peter. "Palau Islands and Ulithi Islands Campaign," World War II Database. Lava Development, LLC, 2007.

Denfeld, D. Colt, and Eugene L. Rasor. "Hold the Marianas: The Japanese Defense of the Islands." *The Journal of Military History*, 1997.

Drea, Edward J. "An Allied Interpretation of the Pacific War." 1998.

Drea, Edward J. Essay. In *In the Service of the Emperor: Essays on the Imperial Japanese Army*. Lincoln, Neb.: University of Nebraska Press, 2003.

Dull, Paul s. *A Battle History of the Imperial Japanese Navy, 1941-1945*. Annapolis: Naval Institute Press, 1978.

Dyer, George Carroll. *The Amphibians Came to Conquer: the Story of Admiral Richmond Kelly Turner*. Washington, D.C, Dept. of the Navy,: United States Government Printing Office – via Hyperwar Foundation, 1973.

Gailey, Harry A. *The Liberation of Guam, 21 July-10 August 1944*. Novato, CA: Presidio, 1988.

Gailey, Harry A. *Peleliu, 1944*. Annapolis, MD: Nautical & Aviation Pub. Co. of America, 1983. ISBN 0-933852-41-X.

Goldberg, Harold J. *D-Day in the Pacific The Battle of Saipan*. Bloomington: Indiana University Press, 2007.

Hallas, James H. *The Devil's Anvil: the Assault on Peleliu*. Westport, CT: Praeger, 1994.

Hoffman, Major Carl W., USMC. *Saipan: the Beginning of the End*. Washington, D.C.: Historical Division, U.S. Marine Corps, 1950.

Hoffman, Major Carl W., USMC. *The Seizure of Tinian:* Washington, DC: Historical Division, Headquarters, U.S. Marine Corps, 1951.

O'Brien, Cyril J. "Liberation: Marines in the Recapture of Guam", Marine Corps Historical Center, United States Marine Corps, 1994.

O'Brien, Francis. *Battling for Saipan*. New York: Ballantine Books, 2003.

Rottman, Gordon L. *Saipan & Tinian 1944: Piercing the Japanese Empire*. Oxford: Osprey, 2004.

ALSO BY DANIEL WRINN

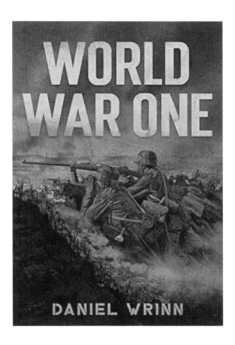

WORLD WAR ONE: WWI HISTORY TOLD FROM THE
TRENCHES, SEAS, SKIES, AND DESERT OF A WAR TORN
WORLD

"Compelling . . . the kind of book that brings history alive." – Reviewer
**Dive into the incredible history of WWI with these
gripping stories.**

With a unique and fascinating glimpse into the lesser-
known stories of the War to End All Wars, this riveting book
unveils four thrilling stories from the trenches, seas, skies, and
desert of a war-torn world. From one captain's death-defying
mission to smuggle weapons for an Irish rebellion to heroic
pilots and soldiers from all corners of the globe, these stories

shed light on real people and events from one of the greatest conflicts in human history.

- **WWI: Tales from the Trenches**, a sweeping and eerily realistic narrative which explores the struggles and endless dangers faced by soldiers in the trenches during the heart of WWI
- **Broken Wings**, a powerful and heroic story about one pilot after he was shot down and spent 72 harrowing days on the run deep behind enemy lines
- **Mission to Ireland**, which explores the devious and cunning plan to smuggle a ship loaded with weapons to incite an Irish rebellion against the British
- And **Journey into Eden**, a fascinating glimpse into the lesser-known battles on the harsh and unforgiving Mesopotamian Front

World War I reduced Europe's mightiest empires to rubble, killed twenty million people, and cracked the foundations of our modern world. In its wake, empires toppled, monarchies fell, and whole populations lost their national identities.

Each of these stories brings together unbelievable real-life WWI history, making them perfect for casual readers and history buffs alike. If you want to peer into the past and unearth the incredible stories of the brave soldiers who risked everything, then this book is for you.

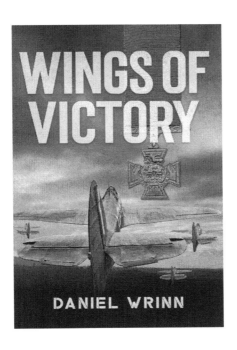

WINGS OF VICTORY: WORLD WAR II ADVENTURES IN A WAR-
TORN EUROPE

"Historical fiction with a realistic twist." – Reviewer

**Thrilling World War II adventures like you've
never seen them before.**

As the Nazis invade Europe on a campaign for total domi-
nation, a brutal war begins to unfold which will change the
course of the world forever—and John Archer finds himself
caught in the middle of it. When this amateur pilot joins the
Allied war effort and is tasked with a series of death-defying
missions which place him deep into German-occupied territory, his hair-raising adventures will help decide the fate of
Europe.

In **War Heroes**, John is caught up in the devastating Nazi
invasion of France while on vacation. Teaming up with ambulance driver Barney, John will need his amateur pilot skills and

more than a stroke of luck to pull off the escape of the century.

In **Bombs Over Britain**, the Nazis have a plan which could change the course of the entire war . . . unless Archer can stop them. Air-dropped into Belgium on a top-secret mission, Archer must retrieve vital intelligence and make it out alive. But that's easier said than done when the Gestapo are closing in.

And in **Desert Scout**, Archer finds himself stranded beneath the scorching Libyan sun and in a race against time to turn the tide of the war in North Africa. But with the Luftwaffe and the desert vying to finish him off, can he make it out alive?

Packed with action and filled to the brim with suspense, these thrilling stories combine classic adventures with a riveting and historical World War II setting, making it ideal for history buffs and casual readers. If you're a fan of riveting war fiction novels, WW2 aircraft, and the war for the skies, Archer's next adventure will keep you on the edge of your seat.

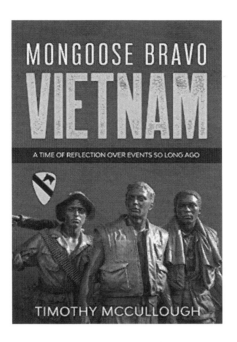

MONGOOSE BRAVO: VIETNAM: A TIME OF REFLECTION OVER
EVENTS SO LONG AGO

"A frank, real, memoir" – Reviewer

Uncover the gritty, real-life story of a Vietnam combat veteran.

With an engaging and authentic retelling of his experiences as an infantry soldier of the B Co., 1/5th 1st Cavalry Division in the Vietnam War, this gripping account details the life and struggles of war in a strange and foreign country.

What started as a way of bringing closure to a grieving mother morphed into a memoir, covering the author's deployment, duty, and eventual return to the United States after the end of the war. Imbued with the emotion that he felt during this conflicted time, along with letters and journal entries from decades ago, this memoir is a testament to the sacrifice that these brave men and women made fighting on foreign soil.

Recounting the tragedies of war and the chaos of combat as an infantry soldier, in the words of the author: "We lived, and fought as a unit, covering each other's backs. Most came home to tell their own stories, many didn't."

If you like gripping, authentic accounts of life and combat during the Vietnam War, then you won't want to miss Mongoose Bravo: Vietnam: A Time of Reflection Over Events So Long Ago.

ABOUT THE AUTHOR

Daniel Wrinn writes Military History & War Stories. A US Navy veteran and avid history buff, Daniel lives in the Utah Wasatch Mountains. He writes every day with a view of the snow capped peaks of Park City to keep him company. You can join his readers group and get notified of new releases, special offers, and free books here:

www.danielwrinn.com

Made in the USA
Columbia, SC
17 October 2024